Crossed Suns

Ian Dieffenthaller has also

Edited and Introduced *Rivers of Time*, the collected poems of Cy Grant, Naked Light, 2008, and

Written a critical history of West Indian poetry in Britain, *Snow On Sugarcane*, CSP, 2009

Crossed Suns

By Ian Dieffenthaller

Cane Arrow Press

First published 2009 by
Cane Arrow Press
PO Box 219
Royston
SG8 1AZ

A CIP catalogue record is available from the British Library

ISBN 978-0-9562901-0-6

Cover painting by Stewart Brown: Babel No. 62

Printed by Imprint Design

CONTENTS

Seasons

From Trinidad

Crossings

FROM ENGLAND

JERUSALEM, EAST ANGLIA

1. Landscape: Cambridge

A solitary house, I build it here:
I hear your poppied fields of ripened corn,
They're rolling like a lone taut drum.
Jagged strokes of blood and rust
Now forming on a golden skin:
Your Nature's stab at life and death
With one curved knife, one breath
Spread randomly: now thick; now thin

Guillotining windows cut the view
In squares. The gentle river fans onto
A blue sea and the drummer, dazzled by
His own reflection in the linseed
Makes for shelter of the green oak – green
Field, God's verdant patch surrounded
By the flabby ditch, aspiring hedge,
The leaden sky – rolls out to die.

Today the sun burns every other square
In this Jerusalem, casts forth this primary
Variation: blue and yellow; red; you drink
This blood and water, wear this crackled
Skin and shake this rusty hand.
Or close the window, cast him out.
No matter, sun is out and casts
Aspersions on this green unpleasant land.

2. Footnote

Felsted by the Flitch Way.
No train runs today, just thought.
No diesel spilt since '62, just blood
Of haws and prunus, yew; whipped
On the thorns of this long passage
To redundancy.

Rename it leisure friend
But nothing's heading eastward
Just the Western sun
To start again. And me
But I'll be back before him
Walking over death into a dead-end:

Who'll take the lead?

No tracks but tracks of back
Packers, back-tracking history.
An iron bridge, ironic vestige
Of a different life: Life, remind me,
Issues no cast-iron guarantees.
And no safe passages by scenic

Rotten bridges to them that says
It's getting better in this green
And pleasant England?
Plant taxus, yes but what you
Tax us for? In Swindon and in Crewe
You ask them what they do now.

GEAN[1]

Sometimes you're snow in April, soft
as newly woken sunshine:
frozen for a moment, high above
the shrieking metalled avenues

to nowhere and for no one-special-
gift, a twelve-month laboured;
given silently as counterfeit.
modest: such a beauty to deny.

And though they labour
at your feet another twelve,
they have no gift to leave you:

Time tests all his enemies

If I called you waterfall, you'd say
deserts are no drier; if an avalanche,
you had no wish to fall.

Besides, you could not bury ghosts
that taunt you from a different time,
hid behind a metal shell,
could you? If you would but tell

Who brought you here, wild thing,
who made you plena, brighter,
serviceable,
hurtful as a symbol?

---

[1] Flowering cherry

Sometimes it snows
in serried rows, in May.
A queue of shattered hopes
Stand spent and white on ordered night.

FAME

I cannot see
a thousand blue aeroplanes
swifting through a blue blue
sky can you?

Size and speed
are relative relatives

And now you are so massive
and you fly so
Hi, are you an aeroplane,
blue, sky blue, are you?
Mm!

CITY: GAMES

The sun: the full sun catches
on the thorny street,
scattering its basket of ribbons.

Towers barcode pallid stone;
guiding stripe-bred,
gentlemen on automatic.

The laughs; the full laughs
echo off these windowed thorns:
the children see and skip between

the precious rays of light-spun
days: when the spirit is,
the body is, light.

A park bench says
that little things
please little minds

while all around
no bigger ones have time
to find small pleasures.

Park knows there's more to life
than living – those who plant a May tree
for its linen dress and grinning

freckles, sing a sweeter song
than they who plant
the hedge of thorns.

and those who crowned with thorns,
but take the time to quickstep over
pavement cracks, may yet be admitted

to the games the children play.

COMMON

Trunks ablaze on the setting
day: attitudes harden.
Brittle branches winter has broken,
soften now.
Mind and matter meeting and
dispersed on common ground.

Time and conscience; yesterday's
chip papers, pricked on gorse,
twice yellowed.
Memories and blackthorn petals
sparkle on the brimming pond.

You don't have to say it. Won't you
stay awhile? That dog's got tired
of the same old stick I see.
I don't have to...
Now the trees are black and white
and clear of wood on common ground.

IMAGINARY BARRIERS

A new year stripes the wooden
floor. Unforeseen, the stony sky is
rolled from Winter's tomb, the
spirit flown again to Easter.

The sediment of self-assessment,
stays within the bottle:
we have no need of drink
to scale an imaginary barrier.

This New Year's Day, our moments
die and rise before we bury them;
our sun has wings. Today we'll see
beyond all seasonal fences.

We say the day's a bluesy hue of
joy; it crackles like fresh toast
in eager mouths. The sky is clear

and deep enough to lose our demons in;
the earth is black and white
in all its colours.

We've spent our years respecting
walls and opening their doors
politely. But not today.

This day our house is roofed in sheets of light;
our floor's my black, your white and built
to span the gap between a day and night.

BLUES

He says, paint me something
blue; it's not I'm blue
but blues are coursing through me:
I'm above it now I'm standing
on death's shoulders looking out to see.

She says, what period;
tell what time of day?
Her body tosses in the moon-bright
blue-hewn night. Her body
turns the heads of day.

She say that blues is a collected
work; a sometime later feeling
Only just in time express
A nationhood of feelings.
Slowly, slowly, you and me flattened

As a third
Flattened as a seventh
Heavenly

TOOTH AND NAIL

Any of the various bone-like structures,
Horny plate of the dorsal surface;
Technically. But we'd no time for this:
We fought like hell to get away.

Old English, toth, Old High German, nagal.
Had we time we should acknowledge
These ancient debts
But we were fighting hard.

Then many broken teeth
And broken toenails later
They just sent us down:
We'd fought tooth and nail

And lost, which left us staring
At the etymology of football.
The part of the vertebrate leg; not
The social function but the roundish body.

Old English, fot, High German balla.
Not to have one but to kick one:
Seems so obvious now,
We should have checked, of course

OUR FRIENDS IN THE NORTH

And yes I lived there once among
the football teams called Stanley,
cloth caps and clothing mills creating
pockets deep into the fabric.

Was I too late – behind
the closing of the gate? And what was
factory was rubble: northern light
refracted on the ash of burning caps.

And Stan had taken ill poor man –
near fatal stroke. But pockets ran
deep, and deep compressed below
the coal lay those reluctant diamonds.

Shallow pockets, shallow minds, half
a brain finds just enough to occupy it
here. Blinded by the glare of London's
bright parade and a clearly lit reminder

that nature stitches up a disused
pocket: every year of no return
might be the final chance to claim
those gems that glow, not dance.

FOR THOSE AT CASTLEGATE

Voices echo in the crown post room:
Spirits lifted in the Crown recall
Their entrance through this castle's gate.

Wavy suns and crescent moons; separate
Religions but the same church; soon
These decorations become you.

Panelled coffers, front room settles,
Panels of our lives appended
To this ancient timber frame.

Newark peeping through the kitchen window,
Martin seeping through the party wall;
Fires burning in the hearth at last.

Then the music for the weary traveller;
Loose funk retrospective; new style
Punk perspective; rhythms worn in old shoes.

And the menu reads thus: houses,
Antiques, red blood wine and Guinness,
Plants; in equal measure.

Pottering and potting up; weeding out,
Building up, painting, drawing (cups of tea);
Burning down night's doors upon the patio.

And our rambling conversations on the winding
Stair, shortened by the low beams: all our earth
Is snug beneath this steep clay roof.

Dodging shadows of the washing on the blue yard floor;
Hanging old black jackets on the green door. Painting
Old blue lias white; making all our colours right.

And still the decorations hanging there
Take us past religion and the world becoming flatter:
Now we're all one church, it doesn't seem to matter.

ON RETURNING TO COLLEGE

I heard a woman speak in tongues
today and they were fast
and said peculiar things.
I waited for my friend Godot
and when he came, he said
the birds have wings.

I said that skies are blue
and he said, organisers organise.
I said, don't talk that fast,
I may not understand.

So we waited for the firemen;
no one told us they were firemen
yet when they came, they were
and put our fires out.
No one told them where our fires were:
we all lost a tooth

But not an eye;
I light the hidden candle.
For we have been this way before
and chance, fine thing, we may again.

I met some fellow travellers
just one road more cynical;
just one grin more smiling;
resigned to walking in comforting shoes.
And they had been this way before
and chanced upon me here. Fine thing.

FROM LONDON

FOLLOW THE LEADER

The plane leaves have fallen:
moulting branches hold aloft
a winter's parade of gallows.

Stay well clear of street
sweepers tidying the corpses
into little plastic trolleys.

Linger in the London chaos
longer. Sodium and smog conspire
with the half days: stir well.

I heard you make a sweeping
statement on the lot of men:
you used my broom. Bad luck.

Lead me through the streets
by the corner of your smile:
it fast becomes my only handle.

Life grows shorter with the days.
Expectations lengthen in your arms;
my blues begin to pale in your eyes.

For now we're balancing on kerb stones
in between the heated traffic and
the stone cold masses:

there's one side with death on board.
So don't pull too hard:
I don't want to choose.

NORTHERN LINE

Two hundred people cling unwittingly,
Willingly congealed inside an aching London artery,
Waiting for delivery to the fat of the land.

And more and more the molecules of lard,
Stinking like an abattoir left carelessly unscrubbed,
Multiply, and are dragged away.

Banished are the furnaces of fortitude that once extended
From those cool, smooth lips, yet strength is bought
In many forms by those who would not build it.

Now the fires burn without, a nervous heat that never
Renders mass to total uniformity. But blank stares unite,
Willing blood from battered steel and concrete.

They pray to those above the ground to send a steely saviour
And come he does, as regular as He who comes but once per
thousand twice, all lolling, creaking, greying happiness.

Thus the orgiastic heaving: bone and sinew,
Stripe on check,
Silken sleeves on denim.

And then the thud of rubber
Insouciant finality.
All that whispers now

Is dust that settles on the wretched air
And one or two quite unsuspecting players new
For the final act.

BROKEN MENDING

Today I ask politely:
(Your broken floor,
Your broken heart).
I've heard the rumours.

Hail Mary, full of stress
Your lord is disaffected.
Your children call:
Their church is burning.

Our father, would be
In heaven, given half a chance.
A litany of smashed
Solutions; old graves turning.

Leave them; let them
  Stay for us.
Rise above it
  Stay for us.
Drink this; think this
  Stay for us.
Feed this; think that
  Stay for us.

Suffer these, like
Children and deliver us
From all you're able
When you're able.

RED LIGHT/ GREEN LIGHT

Under a flashing blue light,
a street sweeper grows impatient:
the people come and go but mainly
go; uncoloured by the night.

Man at bus stop curls
his paper to the feeble light;
a girl flicks back her flowing
hair and puts her wanting skirt right.

A man in green, returns in casual manner,
donning gloves, to the huddle of two;
one stooped, one lying
making dying look as difficult as love.

The stooper looks to tidy her
statistics in the dark green shards;
the light green man attends the bloody
wrists of another bloody hard-done-to.

Reader on the evening news reports
the tragic loss of traffic lights on a major
interchange. I hear it on the radio as the
red bus shudders into life past green.

COLONNADE: WATERLOO

I have come a way from summer
and the setting of the fretted sun;
to winter and my Waterloo:
the night that falls and rises
with the voice of this chill wind.

And I am blown this way for choosing
from the bankrupt halls of slumber.
People, columns, cast and riveted
in rows; worn red bricks and countenances;
smooth white tiles, white faces sharpened
in this ice-torn colonnade.

Just awakened people in the just light
lean on cigarettes and bus stops;
pointedly seek transgressors:
England is alive and queuing; just.

Waterloo and all your recollections,
what's the meaning of your new V-sign?
Tell what history in this new branch line
that runs beneath your Victory Arch.

World at their feet, they stand and kick it
down this dead-end street; the railings rattle:
the silence echoes till it hurts:
the usual battle; old suits, new shirts.

CHRISTMAS SHOPPING

Evening's light is clipped
and frugal; painting shadows only
in the places where the canvas is free.

The sky's on fire; chimneys darken
into exclamation marks: winter's
statement clarified in ash of day.

Weighty ends and faltering beginnings;
so little time to draw the breath of day:
we speak in short sentences.

How are we to see past winter's hood?
How to write profoundly by an artificial light;
What presents will be found in darkness?

We argue incognito in the corners
of this new old master while the shoppers in
their rippled ruff still vie to be our foreground.

And by Rembrandt-lighting, Selfridges, waiting
for the tills, it dawns that one December
He was born for desperate men.

And might be once again. We make a run for it.
Gladly leaving winter and its rituals to the lace girl,
Happy to make do, with only me and you.

LAMBETH BRIDGE

She's staring at the moving water.
Flames of evening leap
Through iron diamonds
Remonstrating that this bridge is red.

It's not the red of painted metal
Nor the red of bricky bishops'
Palaces dancing
on the river of her dream.

It's not the dream of sleep, nor day's
Long dreaming that records the scene,
But pressed between the night and day
A coloured print her stolid walls will never hang

The burning's mirrored in the tears
Of eyes that dare not move in disbelief
That half past five this day, our noble
Thames was anything but watery and grey.

MOVING ON

(for Jean)

Right then:
turn the lights out.

Pack the pens – they'll come in
useful just to point the way –
then, having calculated odds,
pull the plugs on those computers.
Pack away assorted lists of false
hellos and turn to firm goodbyes
to fellow suffering commuters.

Tear the pages out the rule book;
keep the cover for the notes you took
but never set to paper.
Turn the box of memories on the floor –
it's far too heavy for the journey –
you'll need space for so much more.

And go when winter's coming right
but scoop the evening's candles off
the muddy Thames: they'll come in
handy in the blinded light.
And leave us just
the tarnished chains of river
which we'll burnish long into the night.

GOODBYE BLACKFRIARS

Years pass –
You clean my windows
A skid through dog mess
on the cracking concrete flags
It's pointless running after
big red buses with
front doors –
How they fly

Rain falls
Pigeon droppings on the threshold
Smell and flowers of a black
hearse London funeral
Take me
past those fading brick
and rusty concrete years

To that perpetual wake
of younger lives
The Prince Albert; Prince William
Henry; Crown; the Olde King's Head's
been done in by a Russian bar
The bagman trolleys past a little
greyer. Brand new bobble hat

All full up and going places
All other life traces
Pigeon-holed in concrete slabs
of flats. Rain crawls
Inside a trouser leg
Across black Friar's bridge

Tap, tap tapping, pouncing
Tap tap tapping

Hollow fractured columns grin
through newly painted balustrades
A hollow tapping on the the redbus door
Yes. Rules Is Rules and no one enters
NO one leaves between its stops
How are we pissed off
Pissed on and pissed off again.

Goodbye cherry, flower on
absurdly. Goodbye ash; subversive
flooding through this concrete sky
And plane: broad-shouldered
ever growing pun
Don't tolerate plain Londoners
Messing up your Autumn carpet

Shake your hair out on me
Once again
It never really mattered.

POSTCARD FROM TRAFALGAR SQUARE

Light and air
You standing there.
Sunlight; moonlight; clarities of hedgerows
And the dreams you sow but now alight
Upon a dozen pigeons taking flight
High above Trafalgar Square.

Tall, tall buses turn inside my head.
Trapped cars roar; silent lions stare;
A disaffected builder's stuck a pepper-pot
Into an overdecorated cake
And calls it art.
I call it dread.

Yet thoughts of art live on
Inside this National confection:
Thought of long-dead artists and of you.
Now give me strength to carry on;
This charring cross bears heavy
In the rapidly unsettled dew.

Still the lions are unmoved
Though poised for action
While the fountains dance the dance
Of old routine and for a fraction
Of a second, think to breakaway
But settle quickly into groove.

Like all the taxis, seen before
In blackened poses. People shouting
Wordlessly in replicas of yesterday.
King lion, he said nothing in
His own endearing way; wouldbe
Enemy, sole companion in the silent roar.

Round this moving picture till it's all
One hue, indescribably safe. And then
A drunkard offers me a beer (and the lion,
As he spends the last one on his paw).
Just being friendly he was, I could tell:
King lion found it very trying.

Wishing you were here.

BEYOND SUMMER

She flung herself from Waterloo Bridge:
From Ben and Cleopatra
And all distinctive beggars
Beyond summer to the sunshine;
On past Belfast and Saint Paul;
The stench of the persecution;
To where the river kissed the sea
And made it sorry.

All most because a bee buzzed round
And round her sweet hair flowing
In its concrete garden
But some because the need to fly
Would die without the loss of venom.

And see it flow,
The purple blood:
From Essex to eternity;
No overnight in Paris;
The mousey hair is shining
In a smaller sun
Without recourse to summer.

If only
If
ever

PEOPLE

LIVING EARTH

(for Abdo Nagi, potter; alchemist)

Tall, well-rounded spaces
bound by earth as thin as
paper, yet as safe as houses.
Panoptic[2] platters, wide
and all embracing as a heaven;
blue and spangled as a summer.
Base metals reconstrued
as rainbows in this new, uncluttered
firmament of your imagining.

These are your accounts
of travels in a fluid clay,
which ended now, you pass to us.
And we are carried on
the momentum of once-kneaded
earth that kneads us still.

Today, we give you
thanks these pots
are more than empty vessels.
Thanks, that mirrored in
these living walls
are your reflections.
Thanks these fragile walls
frame countless windows
onto timelessness ....

---

[2] All seeing eye

CARTOON MAN
(for JW)

I was born dying;
you too. We laughed
in the face of the sun
about it. Tugged the long
face of the moon as you
framed its every look
in your cartoon book.

Pen-and-ink imagination
scribbling on the paper skins
of all the brightest suns.
Fill them full to bursting
till they shower us with stars.
We're thirsting for graffiti
on these cultured walls. For some
great saw upon these iron bars
that fetter all our funs.

I was died laughing, well almost I
Turned almost cherry last night.

Was among the grey leaves of our
pollarded elders and betters.
Come sing me a sketch
that will cut through my fetters;
wing me a sketch of a pile of old bricks
startled to life by your cartoony tricks.

I was died houseless, well almost – you
leave me a home in the pen of your sight.

WAKE

(for Victoria; apologies CR)

Mother sees a long night coming but
she won't be there.
She who knows your everything, may
continue learning at a distance: who knows.

And there'll be lullabies
for eyes in the darkness; furniture
to be arranged about the voice
spooled neatly onto audio-magnetic tape.

And there'll be songs for sustenance: drinking
and gnashing of crisps till suns awake.

Stay awake; the light's now passing
to you: same old light: it doesn't matter.
Sing the same old songs.
Again. It matters. Some will remember:

Some will remember in selected stripes
of sunlight on the morning's floor.
Some will remember but
Few will never forget.

WEDDING HOURS

Blue car: blue day?
Red blood on red.

New call: new way,
Old death unwed.

Loud voice: loud heart,
Soft word: soft said.

Blue ink, white light,
Warm hand, clear head.

Blue car, white grape,
Brown wheat, soul fed.

AFTERWARDS, THE RECEPTION

The cake, a white straw panama
sits snugly on a failed dundee
cunningly disguised as a cushion.
Till they rent it for the camera
with a stainless sword – a death
more sullied than symbolic?

But painless counterthrust, the food
is soon divided in 5000 parts.
And all repaired, the air
is filled with bubbles, pregnant
women and the bubbling over
of the pre-Raphaelite children.

Toast on toast now substitutes
for asparagus on toast;
the final shortbread sits
quite smoothly on the samba
of the alto saxophone; the
dance floor rumbles

Gently with the echoes of
Reunion / new union and
occasional light patter of the dancer.
Occasional light chatter flowers
in the languid after-hours
coming then to rest

on a floral sleeveless dress;
a flowered tie. And a meeting
Of a green straw hat
with black and white;
not needing to know why.

HOUSEWARMING

Rain clearing. A tiny
jewel of a house in Putney
angled into sunlight. Prices
rising: Girl is on the up.

The lately derelict fills
with late arrivals, mostly
clinging to the edges: front
passage; back door; corridor;

or cosily collected like uncut gems
in the neatly sewn pocket of a garden.

No one waits in the central space,
now crisply defined by Brooklyn
funk, a catenary of books and a casual bowl
of marbles. A glass case of just-pressed flowers

wants to be much more than just a painting
on a mantelpiece, wanting for a fire.

Drinks are tended, spirits
mended. Robert crowds the stair
with smoke in some extended
literal interpretation of house warming.

And when the mountains of food cave in
to molehills of sweet conversation pieces,
the dined are rested at the hearth at last.
And these are your payment Girl; set against

a past of hard investment in a
pointed garden; silver beam;
alder floor; unlockable loo
door above a see-through stair.

These, your flames, are dancing in the street
and playing games in your front yard.

These are your goodbye
to building up your stair
and your detachable steel ladder
to a snug place way up high.

FOR HARRIET

I want the one with the eyes,
The grey-as-a-stare and staring
As a winter's dawning eyes;
The one that never cries but
Drills and probes the skull
Like winter's icy morning.

I want the one with the grin,
The tonguey, toothless, gum-gripper
Grin. I want the one I first saw in
The yellow kitchen, sparkle
As a primrose; gurgle
As a new-discovered sin.

Born to May and blossomed in smiles,
Angel do you scream for lack of wings?
Do you wish to tell me of the things
That make your thorns at night?
Sure Jesus would be incomplete without his,
But is that point worth shouting over miles?

So many things to say and not a way
To tell them, makes this dawn passage tough.
Yet even the most handsome bridge
Is trodden by the rough, unready.
When you're ready star, there's one or two
That's wanting for you, having travelled far.

BAPTISM AT LANGFORD

Another window opens in the
soft grey stone: a well-read
house enjoys another conversion.

Beneath a tall blue roof, twelve generations
fling their fireplaces about; their bold carved beams
just balanced at last on this uneven history.

I saw you pick your path through
primary plastics; purposefully
laid around the old oak chair:

planning from your rocking horse
your conquest of the earthenware
set neatly on the kitchen table.

I thought your whole face smiled, realising
you were able from your tiny frame,
to hold all four horizons at once.

And all that interrupts those massive
skies – a barn, a stream, a steepled church –
we set into the shutters of your window now.

Today we bring you all these things in
our peculiar way. And then a light to light
your window, at the darker end of any day.

BELIEVERS

A child said
Dad, are you an if or when?
He said, I don't believe I'm either
And she, we all know: answer please
And if I don't now...
Thank you for your answer, Dad.
I don't believe I've answered yet.
You've told me twice my father.
Tell me was it I who killed
The child within you;
Me; reality (of all your flesh and blood)
He, Belief,
The orphan I supplanted;
Tell me he is sleeping
And when he wakes I'll speak to him,
This ageless child, yet sisterless;
When he and I grow closer
We will trust you with our keeping.

GUILTS

I've a stain on my soul;
A pitted metal lid
(From that can of worms –
I know you told me so)
Fused into the fabric
Interrupting the material's flow.

I've a handy neutralizer;
Takes away the rust,
Well sometimes – modern wonders,
Science, you know.
And when the fibre's fit again
The outline always lingers.

I've a huge extended family:
Funny lot you'd say,
Pinning their unwanted badges
On my favourite shirt
So though the pocket's empty
The clothes instead weigh heavy.

Come closer now,
My fading eyes sense foreign stamps
Upon the cover of your favourite book.

What? You say your weakened ear
Can all but hear
The jangling of these badges?

Come, be my sight,
I'll listen for you:
Don't you want to trade?

FROG PRINCESS

Here she comes, the blouse of summer;
delicate and troubled by a breath of air.
Winter's skin and hair of autumn's stubble; lost
but unavailable eyes complete her permanent disguise.

She'll make him think she's like the others:
all leg and lipstick as she passes on her journey
to the cover of a fashion magazine. He thinks
She's a project just like all the rest have been.

Yet when he prises out her first hello, he sees
right through her: through to cold reflections
of his own untempered fears, built up
over years of mis-directed judgements.

And being both unusually exposed, there's
nothing left to swap
except apologies
and a promise to live happy ever after.

Wrong page! They laugh
and turn to tales of sharing
journeys till a stealthy summer
blinds them happily again.

RELIC

You wave your Bible
In your right hand, we
Say, "What edition?"
Perfection breeds your
Imperfection. Wrong; wrong
Hand: religion is a wager
On an unknown church.

This is our wilderness;
You may not tempt us;
Forty times forty days
We've lived here:
When suns set we die.
If you must, be executed
At dawn. Don't bet on becoming

The relic in our altar.

ENOUGH

She sat there
Full to overflowing
Till it all welled up through those vacant
Eyes: life and all its crude devices
Spilt upon the floor.

You wouldn't say it was crying
Nor the spirit that was dying
But the autumn of her way
In spreading all her leaves about her.

And though her skeleton
Betrayed her as that type of being
You would not name her family
At just a glance.

It made her lighter
And with winter's white,
The perfect camouflage.

Some will say, it's woman's work
And turn the light out; say
The frail machine is broken down.

But press your face on hers
And feel the laughter
Pulse beneath the skin.

And she'll tell you that she's disconnected;
Tell you that the air's too thin
For two.

And when you let her
She may draw you in again,
Build all the pieces up
Come light, come spring.

MISSING PERSONS

Pack my bag, my thoughts, my tired
repartee and wave goodbye to sun.
Take my coat down from the crescent
moon and settle in the arms of night.

Whose thoughts are clear; she helps
resolve my rambling woes;
we walk where both of us would go

when chance reflections in the gas light
turn my head into the rising wind:
I think I see you

but it's all too late:
the day's achievements tumble
on the rushing streets.

You must have come upon that wind;
I never left you any thoughts because
you'd jumble them. And never pinned

my hopes upon your door – you never
seem to read them. Do you see them
muddled on the pavement now?

But you're not here.
Then night's nowhere; she
leaves me once again in darkness.

BY WAY OF AN APOLOGY

Should I write this
poem in the *first* person?
I am not the first person
nor the last,
So should I?

Should I, should you
read my I as me,
or some quite unknown person?
Or would I be you:
familiar second person,
Never second best but first in fact
to chart this unexpressable
youness?

Would you?

Nice of me to think so;
sorry, nice of you.
Which really's what
I meant, just sorry
But you'd say it was too easy:
anyone could say they're sorry;
which is why I'm writing this
oK?

5:01 : GOODBYE MISS SAINSBURY

Sun is dying
No black hat emerges
From its golden flame.
Door is silent
Kettle cool
No egg, no cornflakes

Bowl to drown the hard-day
feeling. TV set is speechless
Sofa lost and friendless
City is an orange
Slowly just a colour
Now that she's not here.

Matches like the ends of many
Days lie dormant on the hearth
Still waiting for a mistress.

The thought-calf muses
Virtually fat free with no impending feast
Remembered by acquitted bottles
Sufferings of the sweet night dragon
Burn abright the rope that binds
Loosen meaning, tighten minds

A single russet strand, its only vestige
falls away, remembered on the news
-of-the-world, recalled upon the radio,
Ushered to the new dawn by
The door I slam shut for her
Now that she's not here.

MISSING INACTION

I can't believe that you exist
cause if you did, you would be
lying right beside me, book in hand
and reaching for the light.

I can't believe you called me
on the phone and I reported I was busy
reading up on astrophysics (when you had
said an apple picker would've done alright).

So, you've come round
to say you've settled down. And
I report, I'm keeping busy still –
missing inaction.

You might be right – that I'd been
shooting popguns at the stars – but even
if I had a spaceship, I'd not reach you
till we'd gone past Mars.

It took some time but I got there.
And it's not that late
If you want cappuccino
I'll not order beer.

NIGHTFALL

Speak now, child of night for when
The day has stained your silken locks
The red your blood could never be
Speak loud
Of ways we know

Hold now, fretless child – the one
Divided soul that falls together
With a world that falls apart
Hold firm
The way we know

Cry now feel-less child, that tears
May wash the cherry day
From hearts that worship
Other red
The one we know

Sing soft, paean now the war is
Done, the streetlights burn in silence
Over ribbon that we tread by day
Thought-black
The way is now

Sing it in your monochrome
The way we always heard it
Blank the technicolour fear
Of days we knew
For days are new

CANDLEFLY

(For Maggie)

Fifty eh?

One final candle, wickd
and clicked into the box completes
a culturally regarded numbered set.

Tradition counts it but has tradition
counted all that incandescence
Time has now so neatly wrapped?

BG made; packaged in UK,
though labels can't contain your flame
of tropic sun that wrenches day from night

and like the candlefly still tilts at Northern dark.

From Berbice to Broadstairs,
that phosphorescence danced between
a middle passage and a future way.

Here's to the limbo writer, lighting up
the many mansions in our houses; now's the time
at last for going back for last year's dolly.

This
is rebirthday…
Guide us, candle fly.

YOUR POEM

Take this, your poem;
wear it if you dare
believe it's you.

Yes, I built it
but you made it when
you weighed upon my senses;

when you charged out of
the blue of life's quite
elegant deportment.

When you rolled away the full stop
from the tomb and balanced on its mossy
edge, you were an exclamation mark.

This is now your statement:
just too brief to be a story;
far too complex for an explanation.

I didn't have to write
it down. You didn't
have to be: just is so

and will be till the
next stop fills the gap that
you created...me, I'd be a comma,

sharp and hooked and cutting
all the good things into bite-sized
pieces; cutting all the dross away.

Then, it is your poem.
I just sewed it up and made it
rhyme – from time to time.

It's open ended; far too loose
to suit your cultured friends;
it forms their noose.

You wear it well and
don't get tangled in its threads

And if its loud enough
to shatter full stops into pieces;
then it sets me free

But always to record,
this is your poem:

One day, I'll be
your poem
One day, maybe.

STARGAZING

You made me laugh; I thought
you were a little mad; the day I asked,
when you were fourteen hours
late, just where you'd been.
You said that you went walking
on the moon but I knew
it was closed for building works
and extension from a crescent to
a circle painted green (or something bold).

And you lost track of time.
I knew that wasn't right because
you lent me just the other night
your watch when I had broken mine.
You lent your shoulder for the tears
of rain and when I'd lost the strength
you closed the door again
against the cold.

You threw a snowball at the fella
In the moon and missed and hit
me in the mouth. A blackbird sang
in Sunningdale Crescent. We thought
we' d buy a ring but burnt the money
on a good champagne – a lasting memory
and lots more effervescent than gold.

And now the moon is full we'll
Use it as a pulley. You go up
and I go down until we meet.
And if in luck we'll cross
at a convenient star, get off
And go by foot into its spangled hold

Love is full of passing stars and
minor adjustments (or so we're told).

SEASONS

PREPARATIONS, AUTUMN

Morning.
Dust of millions of butterflies
shimmers over naked earth.

But butterflies are still and buried.
Just the tops of trees and people
show above the thin white blankets

and their sleep. Their dreams
all kindled by the gentle flame
of Autumn rising.

Don't you tell me that this autumn
is the final breath of Summer,
that patronising pleasure-junkie.

Autumn has her own flame; wraps
her golden sylph-self
round all living things.

Perhaps she is an 'f' word:
Winter is a 'd' – all death and
dreams that fill the spaces of death.

All the tired limbs of summer's calling
wait there to be light again:
why am I travelling

before her sun? Inertia?
Or an earthly recollection
of coming through a longer night.

Why are we dwelling
in this summer – nature and the man
alike as Eve and her ripe fruit?

The tree will bear again and bare again
while Man grows tired of living
on the cold East side of Eden.

Wake now
you sleeping cynics.
Light this stiller flame.

AFTER THE CLOUDBURST

So sun, smile
The grey withdrawn a while
And paint me flowers
Pinks about an azure sky
That I may think again
And why
The spring just lifts
An aching soul
To glow
And burn
And die

SUMMER

When summer greens, the playful
wind steps up and paints its willows
shades of silver: how she likes to
feel the structure of a season sway.

As the broad and lazy
river forms an even tan,
the evening breeze
whips spots of glitter in.

And after storms make dying clouds
flap inside-out in recompense
to show the very lining of the day,
a silver sun is courted by the wind.

While dusty suns choke copper beeches
white and bake the river till it's ashen-faced,
the picture postcard consciousness
records that summer is a golden place:

the wind's a stranger under golden suns.

A painter at the water's edge, dabs rainbow dabs
for flesh of hazy mountains; silver pins for trees.
And when I note these hills are barely visible,
he says that they're as visible as summer's breeze;

that he'll be sparring with a spangled
sun along this river, following till all days end.
And summer's best painted, on reflection,
in the colours of the wind.

WINTER'S NEW CHURCH

Minus seven;
tall November dawning.
Now we get our light through
bleached, unyielding stained-glass skies.

And the people cowed and huddled
round, I wonder if they think
that pain might shatter;
let the heat and light
of Summer in?

Or do they come to genuflect
about the white tails
of the wind.

THE WIND

Torn between the sun and moon
Scattered far. Small wonder
How she treats me: blood
Runs to the surface of each moment
See her flowing hair becomes the sunset.

Yet against night, the pale curve
Of her every face is formed
And when she cries
The pain cuts through my soul.

Her slender arms reach
Every corner of Pandora's box
Fling cold reality about me;
While the gentle hands upon my brow
Lift me through stale summer.

For thrills of the provocation
Plant me fields of silver maples
And when the calm comes
You would miss her too.

SUN POEM

1. Sunday Awaking

The lithe hand of dawn
reaches through her
carelessly unmeeting curtains,

Chequerboard stamps
her briefly draped form
then silently withdraws again

awaiting her next move.

2. Sunset

Blood of day
drains into darkened skies
and you

Silhouetted there and gently
peeling clouds again
from all our tired eyes.

MOON

Shining florin
peering out of night's black
pocket, what you grinning at?

Watching over ha'penny stars
scattered from sun's wallet.
They're not yours.

They're free and you're redundant.
Slip away and let me see you
whole and wholly meaningful.

There you are. When you were a face
you'd eyes and teeth. Now you are
Eye of night: your own I.

I am freer for it.
Night returns to the factory floor –
Mindless, blindness – sign this

life away. And you, you got direction?
You just hanging, looking good,
or just don't know which one to choose;

So gifted? Night believes in society
but he is old and destined for another sun.
Then close your eye: just in imagining you disappear.

But I know you're there
(my life's your other shadow),
that thought-felt light feeds just on night,

And money's not the only
form of currency. Fire's not
the only kind of burning.

FROM TRINIDAD

KISKADEE DAWN

Dee
Dee
Dee
Qu'est ce qu'il dit?
I think I understand
The reticence to overspeak one's
Case in dark times.

A single light comes up in
Foreday morning's theatre in reverse.
A lone bird tuning up.

In time less than time,
Painter-Dawn makes notes upon night's curtain –
Strokes of pink and blue; suggestions
For a threatening nimbus; studies
For a San Fernando Hill –
Then sets fire to the emerging composition.

A flock of light takes wing
From house to stage.
Colour takes form
And Bird-Dawn sing:
Kis
Kis
Kiskadee.
No, nothing lost in
These translations of the hour:

Under this sun,
Dawn is dawn
In every tongue.

LEGACY

Death still warms me;
a hundred and fifty years since
we gave up triangles.
Now we're all squares
and full of pointing corners:

Oh to be more rounded
on a straighter road.

Death informs me.
Laventille
till Independence Square,
the steel pan echoin'
and empty on street corners.

Time for a more rounded sound.
This time, have road should travel.

EMANCIPATION DAY

Greetings from this new world.
I've not discovered it. It's always
Been here; just that you may
Settle here no more, you hear me:
Massa days are over.

Is not I give up my share
of old world; not we fighting
But that all discussions
taking place in Old Town,
capital of your senses.

Ask to see me in your language.
Ask and I'll board your plane.
But don't come flying back
to this exclusion zone – this little
forest growing since emancipation day

Yes, oui
Massa days done.

ATLANTIC

Sweat and sand, the heaving-in of seine;
the tangled lace of net and wave; resisting
muscle trapped below a clear-intentioned sun:
added flotsam piled against the broadened minds
of skinny palms.

A weathered child digs deep and disappears
in gold to re-emerge with chip-chip trophies –
miniscule molluscs, raised large toward
the pulsing, chanting lines of fisher men.
No answer.

No one sees his pointed palm
is rooted from a gaping smile, which widening
becomes a curve of bays from Galeota to Manzanilla.
And leaning with the coconut on the edge of Trinidad,
he dallies just above the water's calling arms.

Fisher sons and corbeaux scrap for remnants
of the meagre catch, unregarded, like him:
a detachable fringe, cast this way by an evil wind which
breathes a smell of newly-landed, smashed against
the wooden ruins of a mooring.

red on gold…blood on sand…torn picture postcards
i-land taking one back from the sea.

FOR TRINIDAD: A BLUES

Brand new year they say
but sun born again –
Como ayer (we are in Venezuela).
Here the sea still rolling cigarillos
promises too loudly, delivering just ash.

There the posters selling carnival
now mask the Christmas bills, a clash
of leaves from one broken book –
endlessly repapering
the gaps in our existence.

Here el presidente say to tinker
with the fingernails of time.
There, Britannic myth transcribed
inscribes the need for great
apostrophes on time.

In time, a pause
becomes a mispronunciation
of time's unwritten sentence.
Trinidad, church of new day cynics, talking
Three green hills back into bluesy water.

Anything is possible for those who believe.
A drowning man will clutch at
pieces of a broken rosary – calypso,
and Pan and roti – all we ting – if
he but knows that he is drowning.

Wen de I-land hit sea-bottom
will be time to choose a different paradise.
Here they bend the arms of time. So adios.
I must return to treat with drowning cascadoo
And promise good at intervals: a final

Auld lang
sign –
play mas
un ron y una cancion:
a soca blues.

ON RETURNING TO MAYARO

Frothing like the mongrel
from a taste of crapaud –
toads strike back in death –
the sea is writhing to be free
from slick black poisons, clinging,
firmer than the pirogue's crust and mine.

Are you the friend
whose waves were whispered lullabies
to children stowed in upper bunks by night?
And you the siren
raised your white lace skirt
and none returned?

High on shore, a million eyebrows
form; a million donkey's eyes[3] still stare
and millions[4] still are captive
in your secret gold-brown rivers.
Still the mangrove guardians watch:
those thin grey men with twisted legs and arms.

As ever, balanced on the island's edge
a thousand palms lean forward, dare
the world to throw them over.
Just as Hingwan[5] with his mangrove limbs
gave leaf to art while
tenuously rooted in this agitated sand.

---

[3] A hard round seed borne on a coastal bush of genus Caesalpinia
[4] Small freshwater fish- a species of guppy
[5] Trinidadian artist, severely disabled for most of his painting career

Now time has frayed his vision,
do we stop to stitch the seine
or leave it to the derricks
turning North for tourist gain
at picture-postcard Pigeon Point
or painless falls at Salibea

No black and white decisions flow
from corbeaux, oil and foaming seas,
Save Saturdays, when dormant houses
heave with plastic plates and bottles
in fulfilment of unwritten laws.
Where lives are offered: lives are spared:
the gambler never learns the system.

But on Mondays where the Maya plant
once grew and the cinema is crumbling,
who will paint your picture, now
that Hingwan's watercolour box is dry?
Do I, your faded jewel, fit your broken necklace,
chanced against the fitful sea?
Yes I will paint it, even as it painted me.

KISKADEE STORM

New year dawns,
uniformed in grey
and typing hard;
a swell of words on galvanise,
broken by the comma
of a quick release of guttered
rain onto the concrete yard.

One supposes there is much to say
and to record for absent kiskadees
whose trail of bright pink voices normally
might etch the foreday sun: especially today.
But would they say they'd recognise a fault
between the new year and the old or be so bold as
to insist on marking time within this deluge of infinity?

Thunder rolls redundant records into
new thought, by and by remade into a stillness
filled by a single kiskadee in arguing
for resumption of the normal script.
Yet its only answer is the silent play
of chapters marked by night's spoiled papers
and a sodden jumble of the photographs of day.

Kiskadee
Qu'est ce qu'il dit?
What can eyas know
about the loss of San Fernando Hill
amid this grey continuum,
but to sense that this and all
our shapes will be reformed inside
this constant rain of the imagining.

CROSSINGS

EXILED

The wind is drunk.
She tosses knives into the evening
at whim. The sky is filled with blood

and I am walking
home but I'll not reach there
yet, or on these legs.

If I lean on her, she cuts me
deeper. If I stand alone, she thrusts
me to the floor and tramples over.

Has she any house, or is she banished too?

I remember an intoxicating wind,
warm as thought and I a salt-blown
flag above her sturdy bow

where the sea would dance
before a deep red sky:
the living blood of friendly ghosts.

Yet all the palms I have
are two and red as cherries
and are feeling for another fire.

RETURN

Return us to the dusty sea,
the many-blued carpet, tossed
by some unnerving force,
flinging its fragments on the
island fringe with feeling.

Remind us we were always islands,
dirtied from without; cleansed from
without. Without whose corridor
runner we'd lie undiscovered,
never needing to form philosophies.

But this is our return:
the rolling and the pounding of a
jet turbine; cold comfort of the air-nipple
and a modacrylic blanket. This is our magic
carpet ride, to memories of warmer seas.

And years of England's pulling the rug
finds us here in no-man's land.
Some call it limbo: dancing close to
heaven with a good view of hell, not
having the means to tell the two apart.

And when we reach the spot where
the English Channel runs into the
Caribbean Sea, no more can we even
sort the living from the dying.

Just then I sense, a certain fear of flying.

FROM A WINDOW

(For Joan)

Night's sky is broken.
Black umbrellas bob and prod
among the fallen shards
which shattered on the old York stone,
now redirect the feeble stare of sodium.

Yet rain will pass. And sunlight,
less inquiring, allow a cloudless space
to fix a crack in time: the yearly breaking
and resetting of the memory
upon the celebration of a birthday.

Day recycles; Time consolidates.
And from this window
I can see the frame in present-time
through which those years have passed.
And they are smiling.

LAMENT

Word clouds gather
burst
and line on line on hard-boiled
line fall down
upon the open page:
when prickly cactus flower
sweet sweet; now for now
and come to rest again
Just so:
it lay its head again
When every book is desert
begging for the rain
then just to rest its head,
its a wonder, Child,
that any god
would make a cloud.
Yes child:
its a wonder
Storm clouds gather,
come to rest upon my
chest; dark diesel clouds
they rest upon me; Winter
dark and cloudy press
against me, threatening to burst
But not the absolution
of the rain upon me;
drain away the desert
from me

Words are meaning; less
and less and gather more
as clouds and burst
upon me
pasting line on hard-wrought
line about me, never getting through.
Today our page is all full up:
with emptiness
Today our book is all full

But press some flowers in it.
press some
flowers

OLD LIGHT : NEW LIGHT

Sunset:
Skins of autumn sky
are peeled away in strips
by night's crisp blade;

the tortured sky,
pollocked in blood across
a pale blue mind;

a high art transfusion
for the bloodless times:
a red-out for dark hours.

And times you called it fire.
But fire burn and fire die
till nothin remain but silhouettes:

ghosts of distant bodies from a warmer clime
twilit now in Northern time;
needing now to undefine these colours
and with more than former light.

SNOW AT NEW YEAR

New year:
old contingencies
lighted by a moon-blue snow.

December's arbitrary
fence with January lies
buried by this ancient continuity.

Newly dormant trees and budding plans
that might be sacrificed for auld lang syne,
are now repaired instead to nature's flow

and none can tell if time is on time.

This year, we struggle to construct a passing:
the extra rung on life's old ladder;
another cold stone step, descending
to the cellar of our days. So many
ways we have to counter time's upending.
But now that time is set at large,
where can we draw an advantageous barrier?

This morning has no endings or beginning,
just the shapes of our existence
reconstructed over every manmade line.

TURKEY FOR TWO: THE THIRSTY EARTH

ONE

From Black to blue Aegean
Battered through this land of chalk
Scored and dressed and roasting on an August spit
We motor as its people walk

Marmara: the thirsty earth
All concrete, clay and slaughtered trees
Washed white by haze-blue waters
And lesions of foundered maize; sunflowers
Wind between the miners and the builders;
The red-crowned white, the not yet white
And the never could be tatil-koyu white

The plain rolls up
A side of bacon, rill-carved red
and pierced with cloves of poplar and cypress
Till the hills rise up, wrapped in pine
And fall as faded patchwork to the Dardenelles

Gallipolli: the tended lawns and unattended
Tablets form a rosary
Snaking over half a million soldiers;
Not a Muslim nor a Christian one
Just a chain of heroes (and what are heroes)

From Çannakale,
Asia rising: a green cape of oakwood
Shrouds the littered smatterings of Troy
Whence remembering fair Helen, sentry willows
And the marching ranks of poplars
Comb every border of each yellow square
Until another olived hill stands tall.

At Bergama, from the god's own theatre
See that every ghost is still at war.
Every civilisation lies in ruins
From Truva on to Ephesus
Till the panoply of tombs at Hierapolis

From Priam on past Ataturk
Every god lays waste his tower of Babel.
While the affluent build fortress Kusadasi
The hills reply at cotton-castle Pammukale.
Travel down the poison into Izmir's black
But find the jewel mounted on its back.

TWO

Clinging to the valance rippled green
And white, we climb onto the tabletop
And save for sprinkled flowers,
The salt and water flows that stretch for hours,
All is bare to the ancient calm of Egirdir.

To Konya, ugly warren scratched into the earth,
Where drills of megaphones bore deep
Into the breaking dawn, that none
Are unaware of Allah's call to prayer.
He has no favourites now,

Drawing the line outside the silver doors
Where the April cup flows over
With the gold of the Mevlana.

I feast and join the silk route East

Pause for entertainment at the Sultan Hani
Pillared like a Thirties Odeon,
Pillaged just the same.
Now all the caravanserai are crumbling
Every camel has four wheels:
The fabric weaves no mystery.
But Cappadocia where the earth is king
Swirls about me scores of dervish
Hats in tufa and dwellings reassembled
From the stone and clay.
And though a buried people leave their
Churches roughly tunnelled in the hills,
No one makes a temple now
of this same earth or will.

Derinkuyu:
Every track is beaten
By the threshing forks of women:
Beasts of burden cowering
Eastward, glancing West and scrubbing
Pains through earthen walls; out
Into sewers that are streets. But out
As always: salvation made simple;
Picking the poor out of the poverty.
Their children beg and barter for
The fragments of your spirit you can give
But never stealing, leave enough to live.

THREE

Ankara, the wounded head,
Ataturk is watching still;
Watching from the citadel
Where the charmer keeps his prisoners.
And from his marble tomb flirts only with the alien.
A telling voice still echoes in the caverns
Of the Koçatepe mosque; his gloved right hand still thrills.

It guides us to the green and distant
Deco decadence of Bursa; carries us across
The agitated water and implants us into Istanbul.

The deal is: sell your wares or sell your soul.
Santa Sophia or the Grand bazaar,
Who would choose between an artery or vein
Or the colour of the blood? Not much
To choose between the famine or the flood.

From blue to Istanbul's black air,
Two players I have met here.
The merely human and the barely human; birth
And death entwined: a startled symbiosis
Scattered on the thirsty earth.

THE SKYWATCHERS

Drumcree 2000

The forecast was for dawn at last.
Some would deny it;
others turn their heads toward the past

where still the politicians speak
in narrow sentences; spend the murky day
dismantling metaphors just to fit them
through the gaps in learning.

Belfast's burning like before:
a dull repeated orange sky
ill fitted to a yearning
earth which, cracked and dry
wants satisfaction in blood.

This night is brighter than the thud
of day; and years of drought showed off
by craving heaps of lighted tyres.
But these aren't fires tracked by sky watchers:
muddled in the shadows of their dying suns again,
they plant another crop of morning light.

And pray for rain ...

JOURNEY HOME

Dream well child
Beneath the bobbing blondness
Shines a rounded light.

Evening flickers; this way, that way
Burning fitful corners, weaving through
the seemingly robotic hands of those in front
still drinking beer – they seem to know me.

Different dream perhaps but
Here I'm not, not really
Charlotte's asleep on the bus again

Celia's not; how can I tell
The slaughtered sound spreads well
into the evening, thick and threatening.

Suffocation: components polarise

Acid gossip; leaden snores
Laid back and full-frontal bores
The twilight's battery both spent and being

Spent – but now I'm grown without corners
How can I fit either charge?
The nighted memory takes all turns at once
For fear of taking one wrong chance

When the sodium light burns through dark again
I know this gap is mine
And turn to her but she's unturnable

And so I bid her light
Goodnight and know
That I'm not going home.

HYBRID

Seasons change forever.
No more the scientific certainty
of nothing ventured.

Our house is founded;
nothing to be gained from further
stocks of same old bricks and blocks

Two suns cycled are now recycled.

No lime
no ole talk
no mamaguy
No chips with everything
no steak and kidney pie
no need to take the plunge for Blighty:

nothing stands out
against nothing
in this sky.

Step right up and come inside
but shed your load –
you cannot carry meaning here.

Sit right down. And now you reach
remember all we preach
is the erudition of emptiness.

CROSSED SUNS

Autumn hurries through a weary land.
Even stout grass blades
cropped for the final time this year,
collapse like tousled hair;
and glint like steel; recover; fall;
and shine again beneath her passing hand.

Evening hurries, dressed in stars
One last caress of cane arrows
lingers over Caroni, then passes
into fire; into ash; into the halogen of cars.

Red leaves of cherry, wheel
and race between the carmine faces
higher into madder clouds to die:
crimson, crimson, everywhere
but not a flint spark's warmth
about this thinning sky.

Autumn's heading South again,
her industry unsuited still
to stirring Southern vats
of light. Not me.
My tropic sun can't shine
the corners of a Northern sky
blackened by the coldest night
but then, I wouldn't try.

Teatime's sun pours cups of silver on
the silent Thames. The Gulf is beaten gold
and red enamelled over Pointe a Pierre.
Though I'm aware of all those recipes for
perfect teas and washing seas with brush and oil
I'm no drinker nor a painter: my toil is lightened
by a cross-bred sun that lets me see to harvest
sugarcane off winter's calm and frosted plain.